Expert Strategy: How to Pick Up Girls on Tinder and Happn Without Dating

David James

http://davidjamesseduction.wordpress.com/

http://davidjamesseduction.tumblr.com/

CONTENTS

Acknowledgments   i

1   INTRODUCTION AND EXPECTATIONS   1

2   SELECTING APPS TO USE AND CREATING A SUITABLE PROFILE   6

3   HOW TO USE THE APP MOST PRODUCTIVELY   14

4   MESSAGING   19

5   MESSAGING OFF THE APP PLATFORM AND ONGOING SEDUCTION   26

6   AVOIDING SCAMS AND DEALING WITH CATFISH   33

7   OFFLINE CONSIDERATIONS   39

8   ADVANCED POSSIBILITIES AND CONCUSION   43

About the Author   48

ACKNOWLEDGMENTS

Thanks are due to all the men who made helpful suggestions on my first manuscript... Secondly I'd like to thank all the women I hooked up with from online.

1 INTRODUCTION AND EXPECTATIONS

Welcome to my guide on using online dating applications for casual sex. I never used traditional online dating when it gained popularity, but when the rise of smartphones over the last seven years or so brought apps like Tinder with it I got on board and was determined to figure out what works in the most efficient way.

The overall aim of this guide is to assist you in reducing the amount of time and effort expended in using these services in adding to the enjoyment and possibilities of your sex life. By real enjoyment and possibilities, I mean standing the greatest chance of having girls engage in threesomes with you, have phone sex with each other, do you sex shows over cam and ultimately come and fuck you with no other dramas or obligations.

Many other products on the market focus their attention on cheesy opening chatup lines and how to take each individual match on a dating app and treat it as if whatever approach that should lead to the greatest chance of getting a date is the route to take.

Like my other writings, this guide is absolutely not about 'dating'. This is the guide for the man who is determined to use new dating services for the purpose of having an additional abundance of casual sex and is keen to waste as little time or money in the process as possible.

If you're frugal, virile, and have a low tolerance threshold for internet crap, this is the guide for you.

The first issue to address in all of this is how different the 'online game' is to meeting women out in the 'real world' and how you ought to adjust your expectations accordingly.

To save any disappointment or misunderstanding, I'll state this now... Even if you're good at this, the ratio of interactions that will result in free sex from the new wave of 'dating' services is awful. Compared to pretty much any more traditional method of meeting women, the result of desired outcomes online is much worse for each man. That means, whatever you estimate your 'success ratio' to be for pulling in real life, you would be sensible to expect that on dating apps it will turn out worse than that unless you learn a great deal more about sex and sexual attraction in general at the same time.

There are several reasons why things play out this way.

The main reason is the hugely multiplied level of competition online. Offline, approaching women has tended to require a certain requisite level of courage on the part of most guys. Most of the time, a woman will select partners from the pool of men that make the first move on her, rather than initiate interactions proactively with their new man of choice that they don't know.

This meant that previously and offline, a woman was effectively limited to the men that were either drunk, more desperate, or (hopefully) more confident and proactive.

Online, however, it takes no confidence or 'Dutch courage' to message women or swipe together a collection of 'matches'. So online you're part of a much larger group of men giving women their attention.

The objective of any efficient mating strategy is to give women as little attention as possible unless they're going to fulfill your requirements first.

The amount of attention that hot women receive online has validated them to excess and sent their arrogance into the stratosphere.

The worst examples of this can be seen in places like Instagram, where simps gather and type out their thirst in celebration of every trout-pout pose they see. These girls' phones are absolutely blowing up as a result all the apps, social media accounts, and dating services that are now in practically everyone's pockets.

In this climate there's absolutely no straightforward way of achieving the same ratio of favourable results as you could expect offline. You're navigating through an ocean of male neediness and female validation which is likely to get worse rather than better.

The other reason is that offline will always create a greater impression on both you and the girl that you're interested in. You're meeting the real person in the flesh and it's much more tempting. Other important factors like your voice and body language come into play immediately.

Online, any understanding of body language (which you ought to be developing) and the early impression of your voice are ruled out. In the offline world, confidence and body language are some of your primary assets. Online you can't use any advantages like that over this increased glut of male suitors.

At this point, you'd be forgiven for asking why bother? What are the advantages or benefits of using apps like Tinder?

There are several and throughout this book my goal is to introduce you to how you can see the greatest benefits and potential of these new mediums.

Primarily, in spite of the poor return, each interaction that *does* yield the result that you were hoping for can be at a vastly reduced cost in time and effort, all without leaving the house.

If you went to a club, for example, and approached a selection of women, the total time spent (possibly over multiple nights) to end up in bed with a new partner could be significantly more than blazing through loads of profiles quickly at home and is likely to be a lot more hassle unless you instinctively love those kind of environments anyway.

When you get a really hot girl straight off tinder to your doorstep for the mutually agreed purpose of fucking eachother it's truly awesome. In spite of the issues, when it does go right, it is brilliant. Having free hot sex arrive on your doorstep as simply as ordering a pizza is well worth the economical use of time to make it happen. That's the purpose of this book and I hope that you're looking forward to learning how to deal with all the difficulties and issues so that you can get similar results for yourself in the coming months and years.

2 SELECTING APPS TO USE AND CREATING A SUITABLE PROFILE

When we're talking about mobile apps for 'dating', we're mainly talking about Tinder. That's where almost all of my experience lies and what most of this guide relates to most directly.

Tinder has a reputation as a 'hookup app' in spite of the complications we've already considered. Other contenders on the apps market include Happn (which I use), Badoo, and then app versions of the more traditional and original online dating platforms such as OKCupid. When it comes to the apps, Tinder has by far the greatest user base and is therefore the focus, since most of the benefit comes from pure ease of great volume.

To use it, all you need is the app on your phone and a Facebook account to connect with. I recommend that you start by setting up a specific folder in your Facebook photos for any pictures you're going to be using in your Tinder account. You don't necessarily need all of your family, personal friends and work colleagues seeing the specific photos you want displayed on your Tinder profile.

Set up a new photo album in Facebook and in the settings, configure it for nobody to be able to see it. Facebook allows this. Then load in all of the photos that you wish to try out in your profile to that album only.

Similarly, Happn requires Facebook to connect at the time of writing. Once you've got your designated private album set up, you can select photos from this album for both apps or any other services you wish to try out. My personal suggestion is that the volume on Tinder and Happn is enough to be getting on with.

The volume of members on other similar apps is too small in comparison to be considered equivalent at this point in time. With the traditional site app versions like eHarmony, OKCupid and Plenty of Fish the game is a little bit different anyway. These platforms allow the messaging of other members *without* the requirement of a mutual 'like', which means that every girl's inbox gets rapidly swamped. I was once out with a stripper before I fucked her and she logged into a couple of these to demonstrate. With a cleavage-happy first photo, the messages were coming in at the rate of about one a second. When you're wondering why women generally have a blase attitude towards men and sex, this kind of thing nowadays goes a long way to explaining why. The easy no-confidence-required game is saturated enough on apps like Tinder without going to the sites that allow open messaging where it's an absolute free-for-all as well.

In understanding how to play the apps like Tinder and Happn, where a mutual 'like' is required, you have to understand how people mostly use these apps along with your understanding of the game in general.

Most people swipe through the oncoming profiles in a highly casual manner and at a fast pace. We're talking about half a second per profile kind of fast. The neverending abundance of profiles coming up means that after a person has had the app installed for more than a few days and got used to how it works they'll rarely take the time to really look through the profiles they're presented with. It's an almost instant decision: yes or no, right or left.

Common sense ought to kick in at this point and tell you that your first picture is *everything*. Because of the way people actually use the app, a profile with just *one* really good front picture is infinitely better than a profile with a highly engaging biography and a wide variety of interesting photos. Without the best photo possible showing before you click into the actual profile, none of the rest it will ever even be looked at in the vast majority of cases.

So the first priority is the top notch leading photo. This is the first point that you'll find lots of divergent opinions on. A lot of advice and accepted nonsense wisdom suggests that photos featuring something 'interesting' like you playing sport, being in a cool holiday location, or showing you with your pets is a good idea. That's a load of crap. The end result of this kind of thinking is a whole load of tragic photos of guys posing with cats, dogs, their guitars, etc. Having a picture with a sedated tiger while on your gap year or whatever has become a cliche and a standing joke on Tinder.

Forget all that crap. We're looking for girls to have sex with here. We need to identify pictures that are realistic but still flattering and presenting us at our most 'good looking'. The temptation here is to get some female opinions on our best photos where we look our best. I don't usually recommend doing this. Most of the time you ask a female what makes you look good (or what's going to make you more attractice to women in general) they'll start crafting you into the 'nice guy' mould. This is no good. A better idea is to get a friend who's already excellent with women to go through your photos with you and help you pic which ones to include and which on to be the all important first photo.

If this isn't an option for you straight away, a worthwhile alternative is to have a go on 'rating' sites like Hot or Not and run a few of your shortlisted photos on there to see which comes back rated the most highly.

Don't include any pictures that this research and assistance reveals to be bad. Just leave those out and have less photos if necessary. Once someone actually DOES tap into your full profile, you're likely to get finally judged on the quality of your worst photo.

I say all of this with the caveat of still being realistic. Include your best photos but don't include anything that simply isn't representative of how you currently look, like if you lost or gained a significant amount of weight for example. That's just dishonest. There's a difference between good presentation and shameless false advertising.

If you really must include all of your 'interesting' photos of your baller lifestyle or whatever, just connect your Instagram to Tinder or leave a link to it in the bio if you don't have this feature. I've never bothered with including this, but if it's just an addon it won't do any harm.

Along with looking good, it's important that the lead photo just features you. If there are two or more people in the shot, someone looking will have to go through all the photos in the profile to deduce who the profile refers to from who is in each and every picture. In the sea of profiles, this is just too much effort. Few women will bother even doing this.

The bio is far less important. Many of your matches will be received without the other person even clicking in or even reading it. As long as you don't include anything psycho or overly serious and pretentious you'll probably be ok. From the way that the app is structured and the way that people actually use it, nobody is ever going to be thinking 'no' or 'probably not' and then change their decision and give you a chance on the strength of your bio. It can only be a dealbreaker if you completely mess it up.

My recommendation is that you try lots of photos to see what gets you the most matches OR the highest proportion of worthwhile matches. It's interesting to notice that these two things aren't necessarily one and the same. I wouldn't recommend that you spend your time actually logging statistics on what pictures are getting you the highest proportion of matches because it's easy enough to get a feel for it after a while. What you should pay attention to, however, is which profiles you run have the higher proportion of *worthwhile* matches.

For example, I had a picture that got me fewer matches than others in which I was mor identifyably 'good looking'. In this picture I was all dressed up for going to a sex fetish club with four half dressed women around me though. That's going to put off more prospective matches than a much more neutral photo, but the ones that DO match are much more qualified for the kind of rendezvous that I want.

You'll only find your best angle, best pictures within that angle, and most productive pictures from experimentation so the sooner you start observing the results of adjustments the better.

Don't be afraid of pushing the envelope a bit just to see what happens. When dealing with women in general you can be very safe and end up leaving 90% of women comfortable around you with 10% mildly interested in you or you can end up having 90% of women very frustrated with you and 10% extremely horny to find the nearest bed or even just a dark corner. I find the latter to be far more conducive to a satisfactory sex life.

Of course there are limits. When I was experimenting with this and when Tinder had no clear rules in their documents about nudity I tried out a leading photo of me fucking three women at once just to see what would come back. I got a warning email from Tinder and the photo removed. Up to the point of explicit nudity you can be as provocative as you want though, so it's worth experimenting with. On that note, don't put a picture of your dick in your profile. Dick pics are another thing that have become a standing joke about internet dating. At worst I've heard of guys getting their Facebook albums in a muddle and losing their jobs over 'pressing the wrong button' and accidently publishing their penis photo much more widely on the internet than intended. Just don't do it, ok!

I've had some guys ask me about the value of 'Tinder Plus', the paid version. They have experimented with different price bands. If you can get it cheap, it may well be a good idea. With it you get unlimited 'right swipes' which is obviously important as volume is such a vital component. Another feature is the ability to 'go back' by one profile if you went past it too fast or want another look. This isn't much use really. I only use that feature when I do a double take as I half recognise some girl that I've already fucked locally. The other feature allows you to change your location.

I haven't had much use for the location feature either. Before it came out, there were some guys into the online game that would download apps to fake their GPS location and 'go travelling' on Tinder of their own accord. I toyed with the idea of having webcam sessions with girls elsewhere but really it isn't worth my time.

What may be a good idea is 'pipelining' though. This is the term that some men coined for the practice of setting up online dating profiles in different locations that they were going to be travelling to in the near future. They'd set up their prospects before even touching down in their next destination. I haven't tried this, but if you love to travel, you may get some good play out of the location feature in Tinder Plus.

3 HOW TO USE THE APP MOST PRODUCTIVELY

Once you've got a workable profile to use, or a few ideas to play around with, the next consideration is how to actually use the app yourself to make the best use of your limited time.

I've tried a few different approaches here. A lot of guys take the approach of clicking 'like' on everything, with the rationale that they're hitting the most volume in the easiest and quickest way like this, and that they can 'unmatch' any women they don't find desirable at a later time. Obviously, this is somewhat of a false economy because you're still going to have to inspect those profiles 'properly' in the unmatching process.

The main way that I experimented with this approach a year ago was automating it on my computer. There's a addon application for Google Chrome web browser called 'Botinder'. I suspect that anyone running spambot profiles on Tinder uses this addon or some similar programme or modification.

On Botinder you just need to sign in to your Tinder profile via facebook within the Chrome addon and it would show you profiles sent to your account on the screen. It then had a feature to 'auto like', which you could then set on slow, medium, fast, and booster speed. That way you could have your computer auto-swiping through hundreds or even thosands of profiles with your Tinder account completely hands free.

You might be thinking that this is a good idea but obviously Tinder will always be trying to combat abuses of the system like this. I never noticed any overall improved end result from runninig Botinder and it began to work less well.

Tinder has its own algorithms for how it presents other people's profiles to each account. The profiles coming to you are not in a completely random order. It's like going though a pack of cards, but there are systems for what order the cards will be in for each person using the service.

Obviously, you want your profile to be higher up in the 'queue' of profiles to appear on the phone screen of the kind of women you're wanting to meet off there.

Unless you work for Tinder or can somehow find out reliably from someone who does, or you're a computer expert (I'm not), any thoughts on how the algorithm actually works is intelligent speculation at best.

My observation though, is that the system tends to align accounts that behave similarly. That means that if you right swipe everything or get a programme to do it automatically for you, you'll be making your own profile more 'visible' to the female accounts doing the same thing or the ones making the greatest proportion of right swipes. That tends to be the spambot profiles and the less attractive women.

On the flip side of this, if you are making your right swipes much more selectively, you're account will come up sooner in the line of profiles to appear before the registered female accounts behaving in the same way. That tends to be the genuine women and especially the sexier ones.

I've tested this idea out with a friend. He's a persistent right-swiper and I am picky in my swiping to like someone. We both got our phones out, opened Tinder, and started going through at the same speed, comparing with each other. We both agreed that the women being shown to my account were on average much more attractive.

If you've been right swiping indiscriminately for some time, you might have to start being a lot more fussy just for the sake of repairing the reputation of your account within the system. It may be worth stopping your account and starting again from scratch.

There are articles that suggest that the algorithm was changed to deal with the discrepancies of male and female behaviour with the app (because only the men were right-swiping to everything). There are a few forums with some intelligent discussion of this sort of thing, including many threads on the Misc section of bodybuilding.com. Some of these articles and posts might be worth reading if you need further convincing.

At the moment, my best advice is to be selective in your swiping, go through it naturally, and don't automate it. Use it properly and for the most part you should be showing up highly for the women that are also using it properly. If you do happen to have some objective inside information on the algorithms of Tinder (or Happn), please drop me an email!

The other thing that you may notice in the order that the profiles are shown to your account, is that the first ones generally are the accounts that have logged in most recently. Therefore it stands to reason that the best policy with your own swiping or liking is to log in often and use it in a genuine way for a little while each time.

I don't want this to become a drain of time for anyone since the whole idea of this is to get some free sex with as little time spend as possible. Going through a load of profiles is best done in those little blocks of time where you're at a loose end but don't have time to fully immerse yourself in anything else more worthwhile: think waiting at the bus stop, taking a dump, waiting for a phone call, while waiting for your food to cook, etc.

If you're there little and often your profile shoud end up in front of the girls who have signed up recently and are actually using it. It can often be important to operate like this to 'get in quick' before a girl who has been using the app for a while deletes it once the apathy that comes with so many options sets in.

With Happn, the game is pretty much the same but with a much smaller userbase. Their whole marketing focussed on trying to suggest that it would encourage the possibility of matching with someone that you've noticed in your area but didn't have a way to introduce yourself to. It's marketed to the female sense of serendipity. Back in reality it's just Tinder with a smaller search radius and a scolling panel of results rather than a deck of them that goes one at a time. In my experience this leads to fewer matches because you can just be scrolled past with your profile barely visible rather than you being more fully displayed like in Tinder before the next person in the vicinity is displayed. A smaller userbase, a smaller search radius and a system less condusive to actualy matches make it a second choice app at the moment.

Regarding the search radius on Tinder, I simply set the distance that I could reasonably expect a girl to travel, although I have had a couple of girls make the trip from a different city to get some! You should play around with search radius, but keep in mind that you're better to be hitting the volume in swipes in the realistic range rather than missing out by setting it further and spending more time going through profiles that aren't as realistic as a possibility, meanwhile you're less likely to be getting your profile in front of the eyes of the hot girls who are nearer before they get fed up of small-talk simps and uninstall the thing!

4 MESSAGING

Once you're swiping regularly with a productive profile you'll be getting matches. Messaging capabilities are then available. I'm going to break a few hearts in this chapter because most of my advice probably isn't what you're used to hearing.

A lot of advice and posts or articles centre around the best opening lines and 'text game' strategies. I'm here to tell you that this kind of thinking is what's going to turn this whole thing from a nice little bonus load of pussy for minimum effort into a full time job with loads of time wasted.

Let me put it to you like this... If you have any experience with this already, you'll know that this isn't an online paradise of infinite nymphos scrambling to have sex with strangers at the next opportunity above all else. The reality is that things aren't what they seem in the online world just as in the offline, and there are a lot of different things that can be going on with each account that you see.

Your job is to *efficiently* whittle down the huge mass of accounts to the ones that are really worth your time. There's X number of 'female' accounts in your chosen search radius. Of that number, a smaller number are actually real people. An even smaller number of the remainder are women and not men pretending to be women. Of the genuine female accounts, many of them are on there purely to alleviate their sense of boredom. Many are on there just to get their photos in front of more eyes so that they'll get more followers on Instagram so they can raise their profile for whatever purpose. Some of them are serial-daters using the app as the latest tool in expanding their options to get freebies and validation. Some women are just on there looking for an argument! Some of them are looking for their next sugar daddy... Etc...

If you're dropping entertaining lines or just having friendly conversation, you'll end up spending all this pointless time stuck in the app expressing meaningless drivel with people that you'll mostly never meet.

For messaging I like just *one* introductory greeting and a question. That's purely to identify that she's receiving my communication and that she's willing and able to talk back. That nicely weeds out anyone on there just browsing out of curiosity or merely collecting matches. If there's no reply, there's no second message from me.

An 'introductory greeting' can be something as simple as 'Hi, what are you doing this evening?' or 'What are you up to?' I'm only looking to see if she's available to talk at this stage and to filter out anyone I've matched with who is only on there to collect matches rather than communicate for any reason. It's just the first stage of cutting down the mass to what's really worthwhile.

Next thing I do is ask them if they want to come over

soon / meet me / hook up. If that's a no, I unmatch them so there's no further opportunity for them to waste my time or clutter up my list of matches.

Any girls who want more details, or say 'yes'... I have more explaining to do. If they're answering any variation of 'maybe', I tell them to forget it and block/unmatch. 'Maybe' doesn't deserve my attention.

If they ask for specifics *and* if they don't but things appear positive so far, I let them know that I want to fuck them. That doesn't mean that I imply it. It doesn't mean that I 'subcommunicate it'. It doesn't mean that I use innuendo and jokes to convey it. It means that I let them know that I want to *fuck them*.

I don't give a shit if they throw a hissy fit at this stage. I'm not going to be dating anyone here. Dating for a 'maybe' that then doesn't put out is just a legal form of extortion anyway; which I absolutely won't allow the possibility of. Even if they play the 'I'm not easy'/'You've got to work for it harder than that!' card (which they often do), I won't budge. I don't view my sex as worth less than hers, so I will not be making up for any imaginary deficit with flattery, entertainment, chivalry or any other crap like that.

When I have a positive commitment from the girl that I'm messaging on the app that we're going to be meeting for my intended purpose, I then invite her to switch to a more personal and reliable messaging service; almost always WhatsApp Messenger. Some people use Kik, but this (like Snapchat) doesn't require you to reveal your personal number (like WhatsApp normally does), so I'm not against it, but if it's the girl you're talking to is absolutely insisting that you go by Kik rather than WhatsApp (for example), chances are that any communication is going nowhere anyway because she'd holding back.

Some people wonder what the optimum time to message is. I know some guys who message as soon as they get a particular match. They reason that that's when she's online so it's best to jump on it straight away. They're very keen!

I generally don't do that because if I get caught into a conversation every single time a match pops up I'm going to get pulled away from the swiping. Being interrupted regularly distracts from really hitting the volume with the swipes which is the main advantage that the whole platform brings.

I swipe and message in different phases. Really you can have a postive interaction at any time of the day. I even messaged a girl on Happn first thing in the morning after I got home from a night out and had her come straight over! All things being equal, you'll get a bit better shot at it with messaging in the mid to late evening. I've often noticed that if you're both ready to be engaging in messaging someone new at 'bed time', this can be highly productive.

From the way that I message to establish whether we're on or not, I find that usually my messages on the application do not span many days. I don't double-text to chase any unanswered messages. You can see from the last active time displed on another profile whether it is possible that they have even seen your last message. That's the closest feature on Tinder currently to a 'read receipt' like you get on web messenger apps and services. If it she hasn't been active since the last message can't have seen it. In that case she can reply when she does. If, on the other hand, you send two or three messages and there's no reply in spite of her being 'active' since the last ones, you may as well forget it. There's too many people on Tinder to waste time chasing dead leads. Besides, it doesn't reflect well on you to be chasing without reasonable reciprocation.

Because I'm straight up direct, the interaction may span a couple of days or so owing to one or both of us not logging in to the app regularly enough to see, but generally I'm finding out whether it is on or not *early*.

I'm looking for an affirmative answer to the proposition that we're going to hook up. Sometimes that will work. More often though, and before there is any kind of agreement that warrants moving to phone numbers for a more intimate discussion and setting the time and place, a girl will ask for more details or avoid answering the question.

In the case of more details, you will often get a question in the form of 'What do you mean by hook up?' or 'What am I coming to your place for?' or even 'Where are you taking me?'

This is not the time to wimp out. She's helping you make it totally clear at this stage. I then message about how I'm planning to fuck them. I'll message in detail if necessary. To reitterate: I don't budge or allow the possibility of a 'date' for working things out. You should know by now what I think of 'dates'.

First we whittled out the people that weren't interested on any level simply by swiping. Then we got rid of all the 'match collectors' and app validation seekers just by sending an introductory message that we don't follow up on if there's no reply. The next selection stage is going to be the hardest for most men and a true test of their resolve.

This selection stage is excluding the women who are looking just to be taken out. There are plenty of them.

Trust me that there are plenty of gorgeous women on Tinder that will go all the way directly to a guy's house specifically and explicitly to get fucked if they perceive him to be an 'alpha male'.

Most men online (and in life in general) are wasting too much time with mere 'possibilities' to find these women before someone else does, not to mention their behaviour being too weak and flimsy for them to ever take that alpha male status.

Being truly direct is a life commitment. It is reflected in having a definite set of standards for yourself and for those that would engage with you. If you've decided that truly you want to use online platforms to have sex without any bullshit, you've got to really believe that and embody it.

Additionally, being *truly* direct means being yourself. This means saying what you really want and really mean. For that reason I have deliberately avoided giving exact text transcripts or examples of 'lines'. This is not a book of magical opening lines. Such things don't really exist. If they did, men would have found them by now for all their obsession with them. This is a book of *principles* and *possibilities*. When you're taking the position of only accepting what you really want with women you'll really be doing things *your* true way, not mine.

5 MESSAGING OFF THE APP PLATFORM AND ONGOING SEDUCTION

I use WhatsApp rather than planning our meeting through the application because the message delivery and alerts are more reliable for both of us and it offers me several more means of qualifying or verifying before I commit any more valuable time to the arrangement, as you'll see in the next chapter.

In some cases, where a girl is relentless in playing the 'I'm a good girl who doesn't do that' card I will leave a final message on Tinder basically telling her that she won't have my attention again until she contacts me letting me know when she's coming over to hook up and I leave my number. I completely leave it and forget it after that point and occasionally they follow up with me to do it weeks later in those cases.

Usually it isn't worth your time going round and round in circles attempting to 'convince' her that your proposition is a good idea and/or that she should admit that her 'good girl' front is just that. There's such a thing a completely over selling it. If you really were the great opportunity that you're presenting to be, then you'd have lots of options and not an awful lot of time for an in depth conversation debating it. In most cases it's self-defeating to persist too much, and much stronger to just leave instructions for how she can pursue the opportunity when she finally does come round and leave it at that, not worrying whether she does or doesn't reinitiate contact. Only a lot of experiece will give you a bit of a guide on when it may rarely be worth it to continue chatting within the app.

When I move to a different messenger, my main objective is simply to schedule the meeting at my place and reassure myself that I'm dealing with what I think I am.

I don't rush the arrangement to the earliest possible date. I'm too busy for that. If it's going to be in a couple of weeks, that's ideal.

At this stage you'll often get a slight bit more resistance to the idea. Usually it'll be along the lines of her stating that the there are complications on whether she is going to be into you when you meet in real life. This is a pair point from both sides, but also dangerous territory because if you're not careful it'll become the thin end of the wedge that ultimately allows her to waste too much of your time while she sits around making her mind up, or worse, her being able to get you to leave the house under this kind of pretence when she has no intention of having sex with you whatsoever.

My approach with this one is to suggest that I'm more than happy to meet her at the nearest transport stations to my place and that at that stage she can still bail it she has a complete change of heart in person. This is fair and it also lets her know that I'm confident that she isn't going to change her mind when she meets me.

Moreover, a girl that's already genuinely intending to fuck you won't have a problem with this at all . If she's thinking like that, then she won't see it as a high potential to waste her time because she's genuinely commited to making the trip for that reason. The option to leave after two minutes when I actually pick her up is just an added guarantee that things are cool, just like it is for me. Mor often than not, a girl who isn't mucking around will come straight to the house without this stuff. A girl who is playing 'maybe' games will be put off by this suggestion because it means that there's only a risk of her time being wasted rather than mine if she's turning up not to fuck. Good. That's exactly my reason for choosing a suggestion like that; weeding these ones out.

The other kind of conversational direction this kind of proposal can take is her saying some variant of 'What if you're a psycho? What if you're going to kill me?' etc. I don't like this kind of bullshit. It rehashes a load of nasty stereotypes about men that we're all looking to abuse women in some kind of way. I find the knee jerk suggestion that I'm looking to kill a woman quite offensive to be frank. I'm looking for mutually enjoyable, consentual, and totally clear about intentions casual sex and that's it.

My angle with this kind of thing is to reiterate that all I'm looking to do is fuck, that she already has the reassurance of meeting me very briefly in public first to establish if something is 'off', and that any other suggestions are extremely far fetched, just like if I was to suggest that I'm seriously considering that she might be some sort of bunny-boiling cat lady. It's the same kind of stereotype. I'll explain that if on that basis she won't agree with me that it's really a mutual trust thing, I simply don't have time to engage in more of this kind of nonsense.

It's important that you understand all of this very clearly and are prepared to stick to your guns. The main strong claim that I'm making in this book is that with my methods it is entirely possible to have girls who've never met you come straight from the internet to fuck you at your place without any tricks or ambiguity or dating crap. That was an exciting discovery for me so it's important to understand that when you're being thrown these bits of resistance in the final stages of an online seduction that you understand that they're just *tests* and that you're not to believe that she's really thinking like this.

I'll tell you a funny story about exactly this issue... I had two girls I was seeing, both from Tinder. Both had come directly to my house for the express purpose of sex and I'd been fucking both of them concurrently with them both knowing the situation and no problems with it. One day I saw the opportunity to take both of them to a sex party and have a threesome with them both with a load of people watching. At the start of the night, I introduced them both to each other over some social drinks before the action. The two hotties started talking to each other about their Tinder experiences.

They started debating whether it was 'dangerous' or not to go straight to a guy's house on a first meet. They both told each other, with me standing there, that they would *never* do that because it was too risky! They'd both done exactly that with me but denied it to each other, even with me standing there! I called them both out on it, laughed at them, and later on fucked them both at the same time in a hot tub.

Let me put this bluntly. Bitches lie and front like crazy. But they also break *all* the 'rules' to suck alpha dick like crazy. All of the conventional dating rules are just part of a big ruse to get less mentally strong men to do their bidding. Don't fall for it. Once a girl knows even for a second that she can conquer you mentally, her pussy will never be as wet for you as you want or as quickly ever again. All of my writing is intended to give you an insight into the way that a shrewd player can max out his success for casual sex without taking any shit.

Don't listen to excuses from these girls online. If you play along, you may even get laid, but they'll get bored of you quick because you're not a 'challenge' psychologically. My main objective is always to have a girl start having ongoing non-monogamous and adventurous casual sex with me, not to score a one nighter that won't be mutually exciting and sustainable.

If you reach an impasse with excuses, don't budge. At that stage your best move is a refusal with an ultimatum. You won't be going on a date or going round in circles justifying why you're not a threat she doesn't truly fear anyway. You can let her know how to reapproach you when she's stopped doing whatever the problem is and then just *leave it*. If you never hear from her again you just successfuly cut out a girl that was never going to get on your programme properly even if she did wind up sleeping with you. If she *does* reconnect as per your instructions, you've got her strong. If you're wondering why in a lot of what I'm writing there's stories about threesomes, rapid seductions, sex parties and sex slaves, it's because I'm showing strong leadership and only accepting the best of what's on offer to me rather than getting caught up in trying to do whatever it'll take to have mediocre sex with every single girl that piques my initial interest. It's an issue of your masculinity and your use of *time*.

Assuming there's no 'troubleshooting' phase of made up objections and patient ultimatums, we're certainly good to both get more excited about our upcoming meeting with some dirty talk. I describe what I like and she'll let me know what gets her off too. This is all exciting and useful for both of us in making the most of the real thing. I like to hear a girl's voice through the voicenotes you can do on WhatsApp as often exhanging some brief recordings can make you both hornier than text alone.

Some guys might be interested in phone sex before meeting but that's a personal thing. It may be worth considering but it isn't my personal preference because I'm not all that into phone sex myself and I prefer for a girl to do what I want physically in person before I'm giving her the full opportunity to get off from me.

The best thing that I ever did in between getting into private messenger and actually meeting was a threesome by Skype.

After dirty talk with a new girl I was arranging to meet, it came out that she was very bisexual. I told her about other hot girls I was already fucking (since I'm always open about this). She was getting turned on at the idea. While she was away and we weren't able to meet we made up for it by doing camsex like a sex show. I fucked one of my girls with the new girl watching and masturbating over Skype. The girls talked to each other and encouraged eachother throughout.

Sometimes when I get to the private messaging stage I try to really take advantage of everything else that I've already got set up in my existing sex life. Sometimes I'll get a girl to do a voicenote to a new girl while I'm actually fucking her. Sometimes I show pictures me and existing partners made of bondage sessions or sex party scenarios. Use your imagination and play to your strengths. When you've got a girl as far as agreeing to come to fuck, talking to you on private messenger and getting dirty, the sky's the limit.

6 AVOIDING SCAMS AND DEALING WITH CATFISH

Since it is relatively easy to create a bogus Facebook account and run an application like Tinder or Happn off it, many people abuse dating app services to get you to click links or part with cash in new variations on online 'romance scam' tactics.

It's important to be aware of some of the risks out there if you are going to be using these services regularly. In this chapter I highlight some of the more common and some of the more persuasive scams that you will find floating around amongst the legitimate profiles on these applications.

The most common are spambot profiles created to make you click some sort of link. Usually they use the same copied and pasted messages after you match with them. Here is a common recent one going around on Tinder:

"Hey [your profile name], I want to have sex with strangers who are also skilled and very intimate in bed? If you are of the same interest like mine, well spare time meeting me at [link usually given here] and try if we are really compatible to have intimate and unforgettable experience in bed."

These templates change from time to time, but as a

general rule, anything with a hyperlink in the first message or two with any message that didn't fit with the conversation is just an automated spam bot.

In some variations the profile purports to be a low priced escort, who will work for '100 roses' or similar. Some guys find this variation more believable and think that these are actually decent-rate hookers. They're not. Again, anything with early hyperlinks is just spam - avoid.

Over time you'll notice more telltale signs of an automated spam profile in front of you as your browse through. Usually it's an overly 'hot' and particularly young girl and the profile will match with yours very soon after you swipe right on it (if you do). I've also noticed for some reason that often the profile pictures harvested from the internet include a picture of the presented girl in a car. That always stands out as suspicious to me because where I am not that many young girls use a car.

There's actually a couple of blogs out there where guys have reposted conversations they made with the automatic responses of these bots but engaging at all is just a waste of time. In Tinder there's a report function for various issues from people and profiles on there. The best thing to do with the spambots is report them as spam straight away, which automatically unmatches them from your list as well.

More dangerous and tricky are the bogus profiles that will actually lead to a real person to communicate with in the course of the fictitious set up.

An example going around at the moment features the proposition of a sex party. I've had to warn two guys that come to me for advice about this specific scam on Tinder.

The profile advertises a 'sex party' in which they claim to have several couples, a few single girls, and a need for a few more select males to balance out the numbers. If you match with the profile you will be spoken to on WhatsApp and asked to give a 'donation' in the form of Amazon vouchers before further details of the 'party' you're invited to will be given. Do not do this, I've had to warn several guys off this one.

Elsewhere I discuss my experiences of the *real* sex party scene and how to get involved and make the most of it, but these kinds of adverts are not related to it.

Any dating app profile luring you in with some hot pictures with a suggestion that really makes no sense if you think with your brain rather than a dick (seriously... any sex party would *never* be lacking single men wanting to go) and the request that you pay somehow first, is a nasty *scam*. Report and move on.

Another pitfall of the online world is identifying and eliminating 'catfish'. The term refers to someone who uses online dating pretending to be a completely different person to fulfil some undisclosed need of their own while wasting the time of the person that bought in to their presentation. The entertainment value of the 'catfish' has grown in popularity, with a show you may have watched by the same name.

With the kinds of profiles that I run for myself, the most common form of catfish I find is gay submissive men pretending to be a woman online because they have a particular fetish for straight men with a dominant streak.

My methods for identifying these types early and saving the waste of time relies on using other applications and websites.

It starts with the picture. Anyone running a spambot profile, a catfish profile, a duplicate profile or anything else that's a complete waste of time likely had to pull the pictures that they used to make that profile from somewhere else on the internet.

The best way to investigate pictures is to use a 'reverse image' service or tool. What this does is takes the picture that you upload and searches on it to show you where else on the internet this picture, or ones that look similar, appear.

The main reverse image search services that I use are:

- TinEye

- Google reverse image search

- Yandex.

You can use all of these sites from your mobile device that you're already running Tinder or Happn on. Just screenshot the profile pictures or pictures you've been sent via WhatsApp and crop them if necessary. From your phone you can load them into the above sites in your browser and see where else they might have come from if the search brings anything back.

There are even a few free apps for reverse image searching that feature the search tools I listed above within them. These are worth looking into if you want it all there for convenience on your phone.

If you get nothing back from the reverse search that's a good sign that you're probably dealing with a legitimate girl who used a personal photo in her profile or to send to you.

If you're suspicious about a profile early on, this is the first thing worth doing. After that, once you're in the stage of communicating off the app there are two other main tools that I recommend for qualifying who you're actually dealing with.

The first is Snapchat. This is a messaging application that uses pictures and messages that expire after a set time and which cannot be chosen from the files in the phone; it will only send photos taken by the camera in the phone there and then, which makes it an excellent verification tool for both you and your potential new fuck buddy.

Using Snapchat also requires it's own unique username which doesn't reveal your phone number when you set it up. This is also useful if you and/or the (hopefully) girl you're interacting with has reservations about disclosing a phone number early on in the interaction because of previous 'bad experiences' etc.

If the person you're texting can send you a picture of themselves on Snapchat, you have confirmation that they are who they claim to be and you have a good indication that they are happy to follow your lead in how things are going, which is absolutely what you want if you plan for things to end up in the bedroom without dates.

The *best* verification method I use is voicenotes on WhatsApp. This is also excellent for leading things in the direction that you want them to take.

When the conversation becomes more involved, I recommend asking her to say the last thing that she typed in a voicenote for you to hear. If you're dealing with a catfish or another species of idiot wasting your time, they will be very unwilling to to this. If you do get a voicenote back quickly, things are going very well.

In conclusion; if you're interacting with someone and several reverse searches on any images come back with nothing, you get Snapchats of pictures that fit with the profile, and you receive a voicenote back quickly from a female voice, you can be sure that you're dealing with a bona fide hot girl off the internet.

7 OFFLINE CONSIDERATIONS

Most of what we've discussed so far relates to profiles, the use of Tinder or Happn, messaging, troubleshooting, and scams.

There are a few other considerations to factor in to this whole equation.

Firstly, logistically speaking, this is all likely to be more effective if you live centrally in a major city. Living somewhere small means less profiles and less volume which is really a large part of how Tinder makes a nice extra to your sex life. I'm not suggesting that anyone moves house because of Tinder but it would be wrong not to point out that this is a clear factor.

Living centrally in whichever city you're in is less important but is still going to be another factor in how easy it is to set things up. Personally I live centrally because it saves me time in getting anywhere I want and improves the options of my social life as a whole. The advantages with Tinder and Happn are just yet another bonus.

Offline and in person it's important that your behaviour matches the impression that you've given from your messages and overall profile once you get to the stage that you've whittled down from all the profiles and matches to a girl who's going to be coming over to your place or to be picked up nearby to go straight back.

That means introducing yourself confidently and inviting her straight in or taking her by the hand and leading her back to your place as planned. I never had a girl that got as far as meeting me at the tube station for our specific plans rescind the agreement so far. Obviously it's definitely going to seem a little weird if you do things in the way that I'm suggesting if then in person you appear nervous or like you don't believe what's happening and can't take the lead in the process.

You're doing this all the time, remember? You're a guy enjoying variety in his sex life who happens to have added one or two apps to his mobile phone to expand the possibibilities. Act like it. Once everything about your profile, your online communication and offline demenour fits the proposition that you're doing this fairly regularly, you'll end up doing it fairly regularly.

I've had guys ask me 'what happens when you go back to your place or when she arrives there then?' I view this is as a bit of a stupid question. She's agreed to come over to fuck, so you go in the house and fuck. It's pretty much as simple as that at this point. In some respects the whole dating/seduction/pickup thing will be as simple as you make it. It can just be hard to get your head around this kind of notion if you've never been straightforward enough to make it this simple before.

I'll have my place completely ready for the occasion and at most I'll offer a drink and give her time to go into the bathroom first to do whatever it is that girls do in there before they have sex sometimes!

From there on, my main objective is purely to have mutually enjoyable sex as promised. Elsewhere I discuss more specifically how to enhance the sex that you have from the very first time right through to setting the stage for an exceptionally adventurous ongoing sexual and casual arrangement. For now, it's sufficient to say *do it right*. At this point she's taken the time to make the journey purely for sex and no other benefit so it's only fair that you deliver on this!

The other huge offline consideration that I haven't expanded on yet is the issue of 'looks'. When we discussed profiles we considered the extreme relevance of the best picture, particularly as the leading photo. Beyond the specifics of the *photo* are the harsh realities of how good you actually look in the perception of most women.

It's hash. It's shallow. It's *real life*. In fact, I think that one of the main factors behind Tinder's complete overnight domination of online 'dating' is the realism. The system itself is more lifelike. You look and you make a snap judgment. It's a first impression and there's no recovering from it. It's based extremely highly on looks. That's just a sad fact.

If you've got a really good body, it may help a lot if the shot is right. Looks and body are huge topics which are beyond the scope of this book to address meaningfully. Whatever you're working with, it'll be imperative that you assess what you're working with, identify the areas that you can make big improvements on efficiently, and ignore the areas that you can't change.

Most people look significantly better when they lose body fat and look after themselves. Don't make excuses for anything that you can address yourself over a peroid of time. Improving your sex life is a journey that runs from months into years. I'm still learning and improving my life and you should take pride in doing the same for yourself.

8 ADVANCED POSSIBILITIES AND CONCLUSION

To summarise: the purpose of this book has been to show you how to avoid wasting too much time in the pursuit of casual sex on phone dating apps and highlight how to identify the best prospects in the sea of profiles with different agendas.

The main objection I'll hear to all of this is that I am ruling out far too many possibilities because I am suggesting to only follow a very specific and demanding plan. If you want to do it differently and approach every 'match' as a project where you'll do whatever you think is most likely to get you laid, be my guest. I have a few words of warning though...

Firstly, *every* guy is doing this and there's *loads* of them online. Taking the approach of making your profile, communication and options allowed all focussed clearly, specifically, and solely for sex does set you apart slightly. Secondly, if you are prepared to go on 'dates' and leave your intentions vague until you meet in person and try to 'escalate' the situation, this could turn from being a nice little extra (how I like it) into a full time job where you've got loads of prospects in your matches that you have to keep track of and then loads of 'dates' to navigate as you open yourself up to all the girls that are using the applications for other ends.

I've heard a lot of girls say that they could get taken out for drinks or a meal every single night of the week just from Tinder and many actually do this! They're preying on your desire to lay them coupled with your reluctance to actually say so. In fact, there's even a trend of girls making a game out of convicing simps on Tinder to buy them a takeaway and send it to their address without them even leaving the house for the farce of a 'date'. Google 'Tinder pizza' if you don't believe me.

If you ever chance upon the kinds of books and guides that women read about dealing with men and 'dating' you'll start to understand that their whole conception of such things is playing games with the purpose of ending up in control any relationship and obtain things *other than* sex. These books actually massively outsell all of the guides on getting laid that men are attracted to but it's only 'PUAs' that get all the shit for being 'manipulative' in the media. Such is life. What I'm offering involves no silly games. You're offering each girl an opportunity and it's for her to take it or leave it. That's fair and totally straight so don't let anyone make you feel bad about it; it's just sex - it's natural.

I always find that having clear boundaries for yourself is the only thing that a man can control for himself to ultimately end up with the best options for his specific purpose (sex in this case). It's better than getting caught up in all of the other other things that can happen.

When you do end up bringing your results right down to the girls that are most understanding of where you're coming from, it does make it a lot easier to lead on to things like threesomes.

When it's on your terms and your programme, your hookups transition into ongoing fuck buddies that are much more receptive to adventure than they would have been if you'd run the gamut of entertaining funny lines, dates, pretending to resemble a 'cool' guy who isn't 'too horny' or whatever else everyone else is thinking.

Don't be despondant if you don't succeed at first. This is meant to be a little extra and it is my strong belief that a man's focus should be in 'real life' where your real confidence and interpretation of social cues come to bear. Try plenty of profile arrangements and photos and keep going until you intuit which is most productive for you.

Throughout this book I've given a few hints at some of the more advanced possibilities that come after having the discipline to do things in a more sexual way. You will have a much more difficult time pulling off all the mixing and matching of partners if you don't get on that track from the very start.

In future volumes I look forward to giving more specific advice on the whole lifestyle that can open up to you with the direct approach.

Be sure to email me on my websites with any questions, comments or success stories.

Enjoy.

ABOUT THE AUTHOR

David James is an author specialising in information for men going their own way in looking to enjoy an exciting non-monogamous sex life as a result of direct and confident behaviour.

His current writing projects include guides to: approaching women in the best nightlife scenes, getting into sex parties, transforming the physique, and dealing with non-exclusive sexual relationships.

He can be reached at:
http://davidjamesseduction.wordpress.com/
http://davidjamesseduction.tumblr.com/

14017622R00034

Printed in Great Britain
by Amazon.co.uk, Ltd.,
Marston Gate.